STANDING ON TRUTH

&

GROWING IN GRACE

A study in the book of Jude

CALEB RIORDAN

WESTBOW
PRESS®
A DIVISION OF THOMAS NELSON
& ZONDERVAN

WestBow Press books may be ordered through booksellers or by contacting:

WestBow Press
A Division of Thomas Nelson & Zondervan
1663 Liberty Drive
Bloomington, IN 47403
www.westbowpress.com
844-714-3454

Because of the dynamic nature of the Internet, any web addresses or links contained in this book may have changed since publication and may no longer be valid. The views expressed in this work are solely those of the author and do not necessarily reflect the views of the publisher, and the publisher hereby disclaims any responsibility for them.

Any people depicted in stock imagery provided by Getty Images are models, and such images are being used for illustrative purposes only. Certain stock imagery © Getty Images.

Scripture quotations are taken from the NEW KING JAMES VERSION (NKJV): Scripture taken from the NEW KING JAMES VERSION ®. Copyright© 1982 by Thomas Nelson, Inc. Used by permission. All rights reserved.

ISBN: 979-8-3850-3938-8 (sc)
ISBN: 979-8-3850-3937-1 (e)

Library of Congress Control Number: 2024925497

Print information available on the last page.

WestBow Press rev. date: 12/27/2024

INTRODUCTION

What is success? For many people, success is getting the dream job or the house on the beach. For some, success looks like driving the nicest cars or having the finest clothing. To the world, all these things make sense. That all sounds like success, but what about for the Christian? What is success for a person who has trusted in Jesus Christ and is living in this world right now? What is success for the person whose home is in heaven and not here on this earth? Is it the same as the world's definition of success? I hope not.

For the Christian, success is knowing God, knowing God's will for your life, and doing His will. Success is faithfulness to His calling. God's calling on your life might be different from another person's calling. One might be called to travel the world and become a missionary in a poor country. Another might be called to start a church in their hometown. Others might be called to carry on the family business and be a missionary through that occupation. No matter what God has called us to do, we must be faithful to Him. We must trust Him through whatever He wants us to go through. That is success.

The hard part is that there are things that will stop us from doing all that God has called us to do. One of those things is the sinful flesh we are all born with. The flesh goes against God's law. Even though we as believers have the Holy Spirit, we still battle the flesh. We will either listen to our own sinful nature or listen to God's word. This is the daily battle the Christian will face.

Not only do we still have the flesh, but we also live in a hostile environment, where men have surrendered to their flesh. We are surrounded by sin and evil that goes against all that God wants for our lives. One might say this is Satan's playground. He has corrupted this world and has turned everything against God. People may think this environment is apart from any church setting, or typical church surrounding. This is not the case. Sin has crept into the church. One of the ways Satan has done this is through apostates and false teachers, a person who has abandoned their faith and is a threat to the church.

This book looks at what Jude teaches about apostates and how we need to be guarded against them. The sad reality of this world is that we are going to find sin everywhere, even in the church. We must be guarded against sin; we must watch out for anything that is going to hinder us from running the Christian race, not only with apostates but with the overall sin in this world.

We might feel frustrated, upset, and confused at all the sin of this world. We might even feel angry because of the hostile environment we live in. How do we handle this environment? We must first remember that each of us is as much of a sinner as the supposedly worst human on this earth. We must remember it is only through the grace of Jesus Christ that we are saved from the penalty of sin and now are indwelled by the Holy Spirit. We must remember that we need to surrender to Him if we want to change. We must surrender to Him if we are to avoid stumbling on the lies of the devil. We must remember what truth is and the importance of grace.

This book is focused on standing on truth and growing in grace. This book highlights, first, the importance of Christians knowing where their identity is placed. Is your identity placed more on the things of this world or on the Lord Jesus Christ? This is the first thing we must understand when going through this book. Are we truly standing on the truth of our own identity?

Once we can answer where our identity is placed, we must look, secondly, at how we should contend for the faith. More specifically, how we can contend for the faith with one another? This world is hostile. We must know what it means to contend for the faith and do it together. God has created relationships for a reason. We must understand the importance of one another as we go through this life fighting for the gospel.

Thirdly, we must know what an apostate is and how to look out for apostates. How can we fight against apostates when we do not fully understand who they are? The book of Jude highlights the examples of what apostates are and the traits that we can see in today's church.

Once we can understand the importance of our identity, how to contend for the faith, and what to look out for, we must then build on the right things. This book will first look at how we build ourselves up in our most Holy Faith, how to pray in the Holy Spirit, how to keep ourselves in the love of God, how to look for the mercy of our Lord Jesus, and how to move with caution. All these things will help us grow in grace as we go through this world full of sin and evil.

Lastly, this book will look at the final verses of Jude and the importance of giving all glory to God. It is only by God's grace that we live. It is only by God's grace that we are saved. It is only by God's grace that we have been freed from the penalty of sin. How can we not give all glory to God?

Overall, this book will look at how to live in this hostile environment with joy and peace, and how we find success as a Christian. Of course, the simple answer is that we stand on the word of God and grow in Him: stand on truth and grow in grace.

ONE

OUR IDENTITY

> *Jude 1:1-2*
> *Jude, a bondservant of Jesus Christ, and brother of James, to those who are called, sanctified by God the Father, and preserved in Jesus Christ: Mercy, peace, and love be multiplied to you.*

Who are you? This is a question that many people can't answer. If people do answer, it is often linked to their careers, family status, or wealth. We take so much pride in the fact that we have this dream job that people are envious of. Maybe we have family that are famous or rich. Maybe we ourselves are rich and our identity is placed in our own bank account numbers. It is not to say that having a great job, a great family status, or having money is wrong. However, if we place our identity in this world or in anything other than Christ, we are doomed. We should know exactly who we are in Christ. If we don't, we can start to sway back and forth in this world. We will look at anything that is not from God and focus on temporary pleasures that have no value in the life after death on this earth.

Jude opens this book with a very powerful statement that shows exactly where his identity is. A statement that creates a serious question all of us should be asking, "What is our identity?" Jude writes that he is a bondservant of Jesus Christ and then a brother of James. Many people might argue over which Jude was writing this book. Some say it was Jude the apostle, though verse 17 of Jude suggests that he wasn't one of them.

> *But you, beloved, remember the words which were*
> *spoken before by the apostles of our Lord Jesus Christ.*
> *- Jude 1:17*

Although some say it was Jude the apostle, the strongest evidence points to this Jude being the half-brother of Jesus. The book of Matthew points this out, where we find the name Judas, another name for Jude.

> *Is this not the carpenter's son? Is not His mother called*
> *Mary? And His brothers James, Joses, Simon, and*
> *Judas?*
> *- Matthew 13:55*

Starting right at verse 1 of Jude, the evidence clearly shows who is writing this book. It is the brother of James, making him the half-brother of Jesus. This is mind-blowing for one main reason. For him to be the half-brother of Jesus, one would think Jude would be telling everyone he is related to Jesus, the Son of God. Yet we don't see any of that. He simply writes that he is a bondservant of Christ. This is his identity.

A bondservant is a slave and servant of Christ. We see this term used in the New Testament not only with Jude, but also with Paul, Timothy, James, and Peter. The term shows exactly who they are. They are faithful to their master, committed to the Father, and subservient to only Him.

This powerful term "bondservant" doesn't just show who they are servants of, but who they don't serve. If you are a bondservant of

Christ, you don't serve this world. You don't belong to this world. You live to please the Father, you are devoted to His word, and you stand up against worldly pleasures.

Living in this world is a challenging race. We face so many oppositions, temptations, challenges, and discouragements. As Christians we need to stand firm, defend the faith, and resist letting this world change how we live. We need to daily remind ourselves of who we are in Christ and to understand we cannot live in this world without Him. Overall, we need to remind ourselves of what He has done for sinners and to place our identity in Jesus Christ.

When a person understands he is a sinner, repents, turns to God, believes in the work of the cross, and confesses that Jesus Christ is the Son of God, that person has a new identity. He was dead and is now alive; he was lost and is now found. This new identity brings peace to the believer and comfort to his soul.

> *Therefore, if anyone is in Christ, he is a new creation; old things have passed away; behold, all things have become new.*
>
> *- 2 Corinthians 5:17*

Not only are we a new creation, but we are also citizens of heaven. Why should we live for this world? Why should we let this world change how we live? Things may come to try and stop us from growing. This world brings so much fear and discouragement. Yet we don't live for this world, so why are we so scared of it?

Fear is one of the main reasons why we stop growing and stop becoming all that God wants us to be. We can fear the loss of money, people, and friends. We fear sickness and natural disasters. Ultimately, the main fear we have is the fear of man. We fear what people might do and what they might think. It can be so easy to fall into this trap, letting fear take over you. Fear can have power in your life if you let it in. Fear can overcome you and can change how you think about your identity.

One aspect of fear is that fear makes you forget. Have you ever stood up to speak in front of a crowd, but you were so afraid that you forgot what to say? Have you ever sat down for a test, but fear took over and you forgot all that you studied? Fear has the power to make us forget. This is the same in our Christian walk.

Have there been times when you were caught in a situation where fear took over and you forgot who you belonged to? Fear causes you to care more about what people think rather than what God thinks. Fear might cause you to forget you are now a citizen of heaven and are not a citizen of this world.

I remember a situation where I had the opportunity to witness to someone. Yet I was afraid to go up to them. Maybe the reason why I was afraid was because I didn't know what to say. Maybe the reason why I was afraid was because I feared what they might think of me. I never talked with that person. I told myself it wasn't the right time, and that it wasn't important at that moment. Fear caused me to lose sight of the fact that my responsibility as a Christian is to spread God's word. Fear caused me to forget why I am on this earth.

Fear makes us believe that the thought of the human flesh is more important than the all-knowing, all-powerful, loving God who made us. How dangerous is that? Fear should have no place in our life.

This might sound so absurd; how would a Christian overlook who they are in Christ? This doesn't make much sense. Yet in my life, fear has resulted in times when I have forgotten the power I have because of Christ. I have forgotten who lives in me. I have forgotten who I belong to. If we truly understood who we are in Christ, we can overcome whatever this world throws at us. I pray each one of us can wake up every morning and remind ourselves where we place our identity, who we serve, and who we are committed to. If we don't, not only will fear take over, but it will lead to temptations that are all around us. Even worse, it can lead to sin.

Let's look at the prodigal son. This story is found in Luke 15, where Jesus tells a story of a father and two sons. At the beginning of the story, we have one son wanting to leave the father. We see him gather up his inheritance early and journey to a far country. He is placing his identity in that far country and not with the father. He thinks he can find better things away from his father and live a better life. Yet we see him wasting his possessions with prodigal living. We also see him living in poverty after a severe famine takes place. He finds himself with the pigs, poor and hungry. Is that us sometimes?

We place our identity in something or somewhere else rather than near God. We go out doing what the flesh wants, and we end up finding ourselves living in sin and living for this world. When we place our identity in the wrong things, we start to flirt with sin and find ourselves giving in to temptations. We start to lean into the temptations around us. The beginning of the parable of the prodigal son shows how easy it is to fall into sin when we leave the Father and place our identity in the wrong things. But the amazing thing about this story is that it doesn't stop with the pigs.

The younger son finally realizes it was better with the father. He finally goes back to where he belongs. He sinned against the father and doesn't deserve the father's forgiveness. However, the father runs to the son with compassion and kisses his neck. The father brings him back home. You could say the younger son finally understands where his identity is placed. It is with the father.

I pray that everyone reading this can understand the importance of knowing who you are in Christ. I pray everyone reading this can understand where you place your identity. If you are a believer in Christ, your identity is with the Father. Don't ever believe your identity is somewhere else. Your identity preaches that you are loved. Your identity in Christ allows you to confidently say that you are valuable. You are valuable because you are His.

Have you ever noticed how expensive some paintings are? Take the paintings of Pablo Picasso, for example. It is amazing how highly valued some of his artwork has been. In 2015, one of his paintings sold for over $179 million at auction. Why was it sold for so much? Why pay all that money for one painting? Was it the prettiest painting of all time? Did the painting have some type of special paint? Although art is personal preference, the point is that these art pieces would not be very valuable were it not for the name "Pablo Picasso." The name makes them valuable. It is the same with God. We are valuable because of who made us. We are valuable because our identity is in Him. We belong to the Lord.

We have been called, sanctified by God the Father, and preserved in Jesus Christ. Our identity advocates that we are free, adopted into God's family, and made righteous. We are now co-heirs with Christ. We now have a home in heaven.

It is astonishing to me to think about who I was before Christ. I was lost, dead, and an enemy of God. Like everyone reading this, I did not deserve to have a relationship with God. My sinfulness has taught me I'm not worth loving; I'm not valuable. Yet God loved the world so much that He sent His only begotten Son to die in our place. We are loved; we are valuable. We are so valuable that the cost of us to be saved was God's only Son.

I hope you understand the importance of knowing where your identity is placed. We need to stand on truth and grow in grace in this sinful world. The first step is to understand your identity. We are first sinners that deserve death. As sinners the only hope is with the Father. We belong to God; we have value because our identity is placed in Him. I hope we can all say our identity is in Christ. Stand on truth and grow in grace.

TWO

CONTEND FOR THE FAITH WITH ONE ANOTHER

> *Jude 1:3-4*
> *Beloved, while I was very diligent to write to you concerning*
> *our common salvation, I found it necessary to write to you*
> *exhorting you to contend earnestly for the faith which was once*
> *for all delivered to the saints. For certain men have crept in*
> *unnoticed, who long ago were marked out for this condemnation,*
> *ungodly men, who turn the grace of our God into lewdness*
> *and deny the only Lord God and our Lord Jesus Christ.*

Before we see Jude writing on the topic of contending for the faith, we see something that is truly special in verse 3. We see the phrase "common salvation." This little phrase highlights a very important message.

As humans we sometimes find we do not have much in common with other people, even in the church. Some of us are raised in a big family out in the country. Others are raised being the only child in the city. Some people are poor while others are rich. There are people who have travelled the world, but others have never left their hometown. We find some people are more knowledgeable on the Bible, while others have little knowledge. We all come from different backgrounds and experiences. We are all at different stages of life. However, there is something that brings every believer together, something that makes us one. We as believers have a common salvation. We all have experienced God's love. We all have experienced God's grace. We all have experienced God's mercy.

We might not be able to understand what another person is going through because we have never experienced that specific challenge or suffering. Yet, we all have experienced God's comfort. We might not all have the same talent or skill. Yet, we all should have the same motive while using our own unique abilities. Everything comes back to one name, Jesus Christ. We have a common salvation, and that common salvation makes us one body. 1 Corinthians chapter 12 talks about this.

> *For as the body is one and has many members, but all the members of that one body, being many, are one body, so also is Christ.*
> *- 1 Corinthians 12:12*

We are all part of one body. We need each other in this life. We need each other to exhort, sharpen, encourage, and correct. We need each other to help point the world to the name Jesus Christ. Do not think you have no need for others. Relationships are the most important thing in this life. First to God, and then to others. Each person has a job to do, and each job is truly important.

> *But now indeed there are many members, yet one body. And the eye cannot say to the hand, "I have no need of you"; nor again the head to the feet, "I have no need of you." No, much rather, those members of the body which seem to be weaker are necessary.*
> *- 1 Corinthians 12:20-22*

One of the most dangerous and destructive sentences is, "I don't need you." We need each other, and each job is as important as another. In the church, we have different roles and responsibilities. Some are led and gifted in speaking. This type of role is seen and thought to be more important than others, but that is not the case. The elderly lady at church in the pew praying is as important as the preacher at the podium. The people cooking the Sunday lunch or serving the snacks are as important as the person greeting people at the door. Each person has a role to do, and each person is truly important.

One of the most common reasons why churches split today is because we can get caught up in pride. We think we are better than other people. As a result of this, we leave others out. Not only does this type of pride split up churches, but it also splits up Christian families. People puff themselves up thinking they have this higher calling, thinking they are above others. Yes, people may have more skill and talent in a specific area than others, but does this make them better? Does this mean they don't need others who may be younger in the faith? Does this mean they don't need others who cannot display a similar type of skill? Absolutely not!

It is absurd to think failed sinners can put more trust in their own human flesh rather than putting their trust in God, the Creator of all. Yet we do it all the time. We as humans think we can just trust in ourselves. We as humans often lose focus and forget so easily that we cannot rely on our own strength.

We are often reminded of that famous quote that shows the attitude of this world, "There are no rules; just follow your heart." This is what the world thinks. The world thinks if I just trust in myself, depend on myself, follow my own heart, I will be fine. We hear it all the time. However, Jeremiah 17 answers any questions that relate to trusting your own flesh and heart.

Cursed is the man who trusts in man and makes flesh
his strength, whose heart departs from the Lord.
- Jeremiah 17:5

> *The heart is deceitful above all things and desperately*
> *wicked. Who can know it?*
>
> *- Jeremiah 17:9*

We cannot make flesh our strength because there is no strength in the flesh. We have a heart that is wicked; we have a heart that is deceitful. We are people who deserve death because we are all failed sinners who need a heart transplant. Paul knew this better than anyone. Paul understood that humans are desperately wicked. Paul knew this because all he had to do was think about the person he was before Christ and even the battles he had to face with Christ.

Paul, who was formerly known as Saul, had a hardened heart before Jesus encountered him on that road to Damascus. Saul persecuted Christians, trying to stop the gospel from being spread. How can a man like Saul become a man of God? How can a man like this travel more than 10,000 miles and establish at least 14 churches? The simple answer is only by the grace of our Lord Jesus Christ.

How amazing is the fact that a person like Saul can have a relationship with a perfect God? How amazing is the fact that we can have a relationship with a perfect God? He can give us a new heart; he can give us a new spirit. Nevertheless, we need to once again be reminded that it's not by works that we do, it's all God!

Like it or not we are all in the same boat. We are all failed sinners, and by the grace of God we have been made free. Let's learn from one another through this life. Let's be there for people regardless of who they are, and regardless of their past. You might feel like someone doesn't deserve your love because of what that person did or who that person is. I've had this thought before, and that's dangerous. Why? Because that thought goes against everything the Bible teaches. Did we deserve God's love towards us? Absolutely not! That's why it's called grace. Let's show that same type of grace towards one another.

When contending for the faith we need to be reminded that we are never alone. God is with us, but we also have one another in the church. We need to be reminded of loving one another. This might sound cliché, but the one thing we always need to come back to is love.

The "all-about-me" attitude is everywhere. We live in a world today where it's all about self, and how to best benefit self. You hear people say, "If they don't love me, I'm not going to love them. I'm not going to waste my time with them." To the world, this attitude makes a lot of sense. The world has twisted the word love. Love is more about self; love is all about self-love. But love is different with Jesus.

We must be reminded that while we were still sinners, while we were dead, while we hated God, while we were living for the world, God still loved us. The God of the universe, the God that created all things sent his Son to die for us. While we were still sinners, Christ died for us. This is grace! This is perfect love! So, because He first loved us, we can love others the same way.

If you are a born-again Christian, you have a spirit of love inside of you. This type of love should be used to show the love of Christ to the rest of the world and to other believers. The spirit of love is there so that we may be witnesses for Christ and show who Jesus is. Not only that, but we also have the spirit of love to comfort one another. Comforting one another is being like Christ.

We see in Scripture that there are many names for the Lord Jesus Christ. In 2 Corinthians 1:3, Paul calls God and Father of our Lord Jesus Christ by two other names. These names are "Father of mercies" and "God of all comfort." How amazing is that?! We get to have a relationship with the Father of mercies and the God of all comfort.

You can define mercy as His loving compassion for His people. Lamentations chapter 3 points out that His mercy is new every morning. What a blessing it is to wake up each morning and experience God's love towards us. It is a love that gives every believer comfort. He comforts us with His Word, through the Holy Spirit, and through other believers. The presence of God speaks peace to souls, and gives believers joy and rest as we walk this earth.

When we look to God for all comfort, there is also a challenge for us all. As God comforts us, there is a challenge to turn around and comfort other people with the same comfort God has given us. Let us love one another, forgive one another, and be a comfort to one another in this world. Having the spirit of love inside of us brings a comfort that points to Jesus.

When we think about famous people and famous stories, we can think about the 1950s with Jim Elliot, as he went to Ecuador and preached the gospel. He went to a place where the gospel was not accepted, and he was killed for it. Why would he do that? Why would men like Jim Elliot go through all this suffering? The simple answer is this: it is because he had the spirit of love inside of him. He had the love of God; He had the love for people; and he wanted to share that love and be a witness for Christ. This is the love we may have lost in the church today. This is the type of love that we may have lost toward other believers in the church. We need to have this type of love!

Do not think you are alone while having to stand on truth and grow in grace in this world. Don't think you have to contend for the faith by yourself. God has created relationships to help us along. We need to take all the pride away. We need to deal with issues in the church with love and grace together.

When reading verse 3, you will see Jude is wanting to talk about our common salvation. He wanted to go more in depth about how amazing and wonderful it is. But he goes on and tells the readers he needed to write about something else. Just think about that for a second. Our common salvation is so beautiful. It is something that should be talked about daily. Yet, Jude couldn't go into depth on our common salvation. Why? He had an important message on contending for the faith. This is not a message that should be ignored or overlooked. It is something that needs serious attention in today's world. Contend for the faith.

So, what does contend earnestly for the faith really mean? In this book, Jude is simply saying you must have a state of careful watch.

You must watch out for hazards and threats. You must keep watch for these apostates and false teachers with conviction. The book of Jude is all about apostates who have crept into the church. Apostates who have lied about who they truly are. Apostates who say one thing but do another.

An apostate is a person who has defied authority. It is a person or group who has abandoned their faith and is a threat to the authority they left. Overall, these apostates deny the only Lord God and our Lord Jesus Christ. These people are threats in the Christian life, and yet we see these people in churches all throughout the world. They have crept in professing to believe in the Lord Jesus Christ but have never truly been saved.

Many people mistake all unbelievers as apostates. These two groups are both unsaved. However, not all unbelievers are apostates. Let me explain. Imagine you bring a friend to church who has never heard the gospel. They have no knowledge of the Bible and are just interested in seeing what their friend talks about. This is not an apostate. Or imagine there is a person who has gone to church before and understands the gospel but tells the church they just can't fully believe in God yet. Does that make them an apostate? Well, the simple answer is no.

Just like false teachers, true apostates say one thing but do another. Apostates claim to be believers, but they are not filled with the Spirit. They are in the church but are making divisions and not building up the church. In the next two chapters we will see more about these apostates and what kind of traits they have. However, you can already see the dangers in these apostates, and how important it must be to keep careful watch.

The faith is being attacked in today's world. The gospel is being changed to something that is not true. Christians need to fight; we need to understand what truth is and what truth is not. Christians need to understand that contending for the faith means that we not only watch out for threats and hazards, but we stand on truth and grow in grace with one another.

THREE

HISTORY OF THE APOSTATES

> *Jude 1:5-7*
> *But I want to remind you, though you once knew this, that the Lord, having saved the people out of the land of Egypt, afterward destroyed those who did not believe. And the angels who did not keep their proper domain, but left their own abode, He has reserved in everlasting chains under darkness for the judgment of the great day; as Sodom and Gomorrah, and the cities around them in a similar manner to these, having given themselves over to sexual immorality and gone after strange flesh, are set forth as an example, suffering the vengeance of eternal fire.*

To understand these apostates, Jude goes back in time and writes about three examples that we see in the Old Testament. Jude writes about the unbelieving Israelites, the angels that sinned, and the people of Sodom and Gomorrah. These three examples show some of the characteristics of an apostate and how God chooses to deal with them.

The first example is the unbelieving Israelites. We can read about this in Numbers. The people complained even though God had provided for them and rescued them out of the land of Egypt. Numbers chapter 11 shows how these people complained.

> *Now the mixed multitude who were among them*
> *yielded to intense craving; so, the children of Israel also*
> *wept again and said: "Who will give us meat to eat?*
> *- Numbers 11:4*

God had rescued them and provided manna to eat, yet they still complained. Just like the apostates in today's world, they are grumblers and complainers (Jude 1:16).

The second example we see in Jude is the angels that sinned. Second Peter also mentions the angels that sinned when referring to false teachers.

> *For if God did not spare the angels who sinned but cast*
> *them down to hell and delivered them into chains of*
> *darkness, to be reserved for judgment.*
> *- 2 Peter 2:4*

These verses are most likely referring to when Satan took a third of the angels with him during the rebellion in heaven. Some will say the word "stars" refers to the angels that sinned in Revelation 12:4. A third of the stars came down from heaven. This is a great example of what will happen to all apostates. They will end up with Satan for all of eternity.

The third and final example we see in Jude is all about Sodom and Gomorrah. This example shows the sinfulness and gross immorality of the people. We also see this in 2 Peter.

> *And turning the cities of Sodom and Gomorrah into*
> *ashes, condemned them to destruction, making them*
> *an example to those who afterward would live ungodly.*
> *- 2 Peter 2:6*

Sodom and Gomorrah is a story where the men had problems with sexual immorality, and more specifically homosexuality. We read about men that had gone after strange flesh. The meaning behind the phrase "strange flesh" is used to show that this was never God's order. It is the opposite of what God wanted: it is strange and outside of God's law.

This type of sin is especially being advocated amongst people living for this world. There is gay pride month, and companies supporting this type of sin. There are movies and television shows providing content that is telling kids it is okay. Even scarier, this has crept into the church. Pastors are now preaching it is okay to live this way. Churches now have rainbow flags, not to show the promise of God with Noah and the ark, but to support this lifestyle.

Of course, we need to love all people. We need to walk with one another and help them along with any problem they face. This includes people who struggle with homosexuality. I believe the church today has poorly handled this. It has either been handled with hate for the person or to the other extreme with total acceptance of the sin.

As a church, we cannot allow this type of lifestyle. We cannot accept this as the will of God because it goes against what God has ordered. But at the same time, we can have love for the person by correcting them and showing them Scripture. We can preach to them daily and show them who Jesus is. Love everyone but hate the sin in which they are living.

There is a difference between loving a person and accepting their lifestyle. One can love another but not allow their sinful ways to creep into the church. Believers need to stand up for the truth of the Word with love, even if the world goes against them. Unfortunately, churches around the world care more about what the world thinks than God. Accepting this type of sin is going away from the will of God. This type of sin is not strange to the world anymore. Yet to God, it goes against what he has commanded.

All three examples show that these three types of people went against what God had commanded them to do. The unbelieving Israelites should have never complained. They should have trusted in God and been thankful for what God had provided. The angels should have never sinned. They should have never fallen with Satan, but they went against God's order. The people of Sodom and Gomorrah should have never given into sexual sin, and yet they gave in and did the opposite of what God ordered. All these examples show rebellion against God.

Not only do these examples show how they rebelled, but they also show what God does to these types of people. God destroyed those who did not believe as shown by the unbelieving Israelites.

> *The carcasses of you who have complained against Me shall fall in this wilderness, all of you who were numbered, according to your entire number, from twenty years old and above. Except for Caleb the son of Jephunneh and Joshua the son of Nun, you shall by no means enter the land which I swore I would make you dwell in.*
>
> *- Numbers 14:29-30*

We also looked earlier at how God did not spare the angels that sinned but cast them down to hell. He has reserved a place for them.

> *The devil, who deceived them, was cast into the lake of fire and brimstone where the beast and the false prophet are. And they will be tormented day and night forever and ever.*
>
> *- Revelation 20:10*

Finally, we see the punishment of Sodom and Gomorrah. God rained down brimstone and fire out of the heavens. He punished the cities.

> *Then the Lord rained brimstone and fire on Sodom*
> *and Gomorrah, from the Lord out of the heavens.*
> *So, He overthrew those cities, all the plain, all the*
> *inhabitants of the cities, and what grew on the ground.*
> *- Genesis 19:24-25*

In the church we preach a lot about God's love, and rightly so. We can spend days, weeks, and years talking about the love of God and His grace and mercy. He is a God who loves everyone and wants everyone to know Him. However, He is also a God of righteousness and justice. He hates sin, and we cannot be in His presence with sin. That is why He sent His only Son to be put on a cross. Jesus took all the sin of the world on His shoulders. To those who have accepted His gift, we have been saved. We have become righteous, not because of what we did but what Christ did. The sad reality is that many will reject the gift God has given. They will be punished just like the unbelieving Israelites, the angels that sinned, and the cities of Sodom and Gomorrah. They will rebel against God, and the result of that is hell.

Do we understand the seriousness of these three examples? Do we see and understand the seriousness of rebelling against God, and going against what God has ordered? God loves everyone and has provided a way for salvation. We just need to accept the gift. Stand on truth and grow in grace.

FOUR

TRAITS OF THE APOSTATES

> *Jude 1:8*
> *Likewise, also these dreamers defile the flesh, reject*
> *authority, and speak evil of dignitaries.*

The book of Jude lists a range of traits that apostates have, from verse 8 to verse 19. As we go through these traits, keep in mind what we see in churches today. In previous chapters, we have talked about how apostates have crept in the church. The sad reality is that these people cause division and try to stop the work of the Lord. What Jude saw about these apostates in his time is very similar to what we see in our time.

Right from verse 8 we see three traits of these apostates. They are dreamers that defile the flesh, reject authority, and speak evil of dignitaries. First, they are dreamers that defile the flesh. The two main reasons why I think Jude writes that apostates are dreamers is that their thoughts are poisoned, and they also use so-called "spiritual visions" to make their case on why they do certain things. People may say they've had a vision or dream from God but twist the meaning for their own gain. It is not to say God can't speak through dreams. This happens. However, these apostates have claimed falsely that God is calling them to do something because of a dream. Overall, these apostates think and live in their own world and ultimately dream about how they can give in to their sinful cravings.

The second trait we see in verse 8 is that apostates reject authority. They go against what God has ordained and what God has planned. This links back to the three examples in chapter 3. Do we see people rejecting authority in the church today? Maybe rejecting the authority of a pastor or elder? Ultimately, these apostates have rejected God's authority. They have rejected what God has commanded. As you keep reading the book of Jude, you will see the mention of rejecting authority again. This is a clear sign of what an apostate is. They are not submissive to the Father and to the church. It reminds me of the devil. Right from the beginning, Lucifer couldn't handle being under someone else's authority. Pride took control. This is also true for the apostate.

The third trait we see in verse 8 is that they speak evil against dignitaries. Apostates will talk evil about people of power in the divine, angelic, or human nature. This leads into verse 9 where Michael the archangel is contending with the devil. This is when they disputed over the body of Moses. We will look more into that later in the chapter, but for now let's look more at the traits of the apostates.

> *But these speak evil of whatever they do not know;*
> *and whatever they know naturally, like brute beasts,*
> *in these things they corrupt themselves.*
> *- Jude 1:10*

In verse 10, the apostates also speak evil of whatever they do not know. We read in verse 19 that apostates do not have the spirit, meaning they cannot understand truth like believers can. There are churches today where false teachers and apostates cannot understand the truth of what the gospel really is. They are ignorant. They are unaware and speak on things they cannot understand. How sad that is.

How sad that we live in a world full of false teachers and apostates who only understand what they know naturally, like brute beasts. This shows that apostates cannot understand what God wanted humans to understand. They are dreamers that focus on sin and not on the truth of the gospel. They focus on themselves and cannot understand the things of God. At the end of verse 10, we see that while doing these things, apostates corrupt themselves and nothing good comes from this. Can we see this in today's world?

Jude continues by giving biblical examples of similar wickedness.

> *Woe to them! For they have gone in the way of Cain,*
> *have run greedily in the error of Balaam for profit, and*
> *perished in the rebellion of Korah.*
> *- Jude 1:11*

The first example in verse 11 is Cain. We understand that Cain and Abel offered sacrifices to God. Cain offered vegetables; Abel offered the firstborn of his flock. We read in Genesis that God rejected the offering that Cain gave. The meaning behind God's rejection of Cain was that through Abel's faith he offered blood sacrifice by giving God the firstborn of his flock. You can say Cain created his own way to worship God and not what God wanted. This is the same with apostates. They create new ways that seem okay but to God it is not true worship. True worship comes from the heart, and true worship is when a person comes to obey what God has called him or her to do.

The next example in verse 11 is Balaam. The prophet is seen first in Numbers 22. During the Israelites' journey, Balac, who was the king of Moab, asked Balaam to curse Israel. After Balaam said no, the king of Moab offered Balaam more money. Balaam accepted the offer. The point here is that Balaam valued money over God. Balaam thought of personal wealth rather than the Israelites. Do we see this in the church today where church leaders focus only on the numbers and financial gain? It is sad to see churches that only care about money rather than the souls of men and women.

The final example in verse 11 is Korah. We read about him in Numbers. Korah and others rejected the authority of Moses. They rebelled not only against Moses but ultimately rejected God's authority. God ended up destroying those who went against His authority. This once again is an example of how apostates are those that rebel against authority. God will punish these people.

> *These are spots in your love feasts, while they feast with you without fear, serving only themselves. They are clouds without water, carried about by the winds; late autumn trees without fruit, twice dead, pulled up by the roots.*
>
> *- Jude 1:12*

Here in verse 12, we have Jude describing apostates in a more unique way. The first trait we see in verse 12 is that they "are spots in the love feasts, while they feast with you without fear." The love feast mentioned in Jude is when the early church would gather for food and fellowship. Although we see other verses mentioning believers in the Bible gathering in this way, Jude describes it as the "love feast."

This gathering is to promote unity and fellowship with other believers. The love feast was most likely a shared meal, much like what we would call a potluck today. However, apostates today are eating at love feasts. They are taking advantage of believers and gathering with them, they are there but not in true fellowship with them.

By definition, the breaking of bread or communion could be considered a form of the love feast. This is because during communion believers gather to take the bread and cup symbolising Christ's body broken and blood shed on the cross. Jude however is likely referring to a more general sharing of a meal. Either way, these apostates are spots in the love feast. Their selfishness ruins the meals that are supposed to bring unity.

It is interesting that we see the word fear in verse 12 also. Apostates have no fear of God. Do we see that in today's world? The fear of God has gone away. People do not fear what God can do. They don't have a fear that is a fear of surrendering to Him. It is scary when you see people live this way. They should fear the all-powerful, mighty God.

We also see in verse 12 that they serve only themselves. In today's church, we see people who do not care about the members in the church. They walk around thinking only about themselves, living like the world revolves around them. They go into church thinking about how they can benefit from this. They do not think about true worship and the idea of helping a brother or sister in Christ. Once again, we see the theme of pride.

The third trait we see in verse 12 is that apostates are clouds without water. Have you ever sat outside looking at the clouds? Maybe looking for the rain when it's been a dry season, but nothing happens? You expect rain and yet the winds carry the clouds away. This is the idea. They hold promise, and nothing happens. This is like the apostates. They hold promise, they speak on things and say the right things at the time, but nothing happens. Their actions do not produce a Godly person.

Lastly, we see in verse 12 that apostates are late autumn trees without fruit, twice dead, and pulled up by the roots. Apostates produce nothing good. They are pulled up by the roots, meaning they don't have any life. We must remember that apostates do not have the Spirit. How can we expect these people to have life when they are not filled with the only thing that gives true life?

> *Raging waves of the sea, foaming up their own shame;*
> *wandering stars for whom is reserved the blackness of*
> *darkness forever.*
>
> *- Jude 1:13*

Jude continues with more unique traits in verse 13. The idea in verse 13 is that apostates are raging waves of the sea that foam up their own shame, meaning that apostates only show shame. Waves can be loud; waves can make a lot of noise. It is the same with apostates and false teachers. They make a lot of sound, talking about things they don't really know, and yet the only result they show is shame.

The other trait in verse 13 is that apostates are wandering stars for whom is reserved the blackness of darkness forever. The idea here is that you can't follow a star that is wandering. You can't truly follow false teachers and apostates who are not filled with the Spirit. You can't follow these people because it will lead you astray; you will be led to destruction and shame. Do we see this in today's world? What a shame when we see people who are led astray by apostates.

Once again, we must understand that these people are without the Spirit, meaning they are ungodly.

> *Now Enoch, the seventh from Adam, prophesied about these men also, saying, "Behold, the Lord comes with ten thousand of His saints, to execute judgment on all, to convict all who are ungodly among them of all their ungodly deeds which they have committed in an ungodly way, and of all the harsh things which ungodly sinners have spoken against Him.*
>
> *- Jude 1:14-15*

We see the word 'ungodly' 4 times in these verses. Everything these apostates do is ungodly and unpleasant to the Father.

> *These are grumblers, complainers, walking according to their own lusts; and they mouth great swelling words, flattering people to gain advantage.*
>
> *- Jude 1:16*

Verse 16 carries on with 3 more traits: apostates are grumblers and complainers, walking in their own lusts, and they know the art of flattery.

Apostates will always grumble and complain. Apostates will always look at the bad and negative without looking at what God has provided for them. True believers in Christ will be thankful. They will appreciate the good and give God praise. One of the best examples of God's people who complained instead of being thankful is the Israelites in the wilderness. This is one of the examples mentioned in verses 5-7. The people complained even though God had provided for them and rescued them out of the land of Egypt. Even if you are a true believer in Christ, this can be hard. We can focus so much on the negatives, and it can be easy to complain. However, Christians shouldn't be this way. This is a clear trait of an apostate and not a Christian.

Apostates also walk in their own lust. They live to please their own desires and not God's. They give in to their own wants and walk in their own filthiness. Lastly, we see in verse 16 that apostates know the art of flattery. They know how to talk with people to win them over. They know how to please man. This is one reason why false teachers can have big crowds. They know what to say to please man and not God. Just think about churches that only speak on love and not judgment, that speak on wealth and not suffering. False teachers and apostates will tell you what you want to hear, not what you need to hear.

> *How they told you that there would be mockers in the last time who would walk according to their own ungodly lusts. These are sensual persons, who cause divisions, not having the Spirit.*
>
> *- Jude 1:18-19*

The last few traits we see in Jude are found in verses 18 and 19. Apostates are mockers causing division, and they do not have the Spirit.

The sad truth is that apostates are scoffers who mock the truth of God but praise their own sinful lusts. If we go all the way back to verse 10, we see that apostates speak evil of whatever they do not know. Apostates will mock and speak evil of the truth and the Spirit because, ultimately, they don't have the Spirit. This is dangerous when apostates are in the church. Why? They cause divisions.

There are so many churches that are fighting divisions. So many churches cannot come together. Instead, they fight over little and useless things that really do not matter. The word pride comes to mind when looking at this. People want to be right; they want to please themselves, and they forget what the church is about. The church is about pleasing God, spreading God's word, saving the lost, and building one another up. When pride gets in the way, divisions start. For Christians this can be hard. We can be too easily focused on small aspects of church and create divisions rather than focus on Jesus. We must be different from these apostates. Apostates only cause trouble. When they speak in the church, they only cause division because they speak on things they do not know; They mock the truth; and they lead people astray.

Overall, we see time and time again that these apostates do not have the Spirit. Apostates have come into the church and influenced many. They have crept into the church and have used flattery to please others. Why are they so dangerous? They are causing division because they deliver false truths that make people stumble. They take people away from the true word of God.

To summarize, verses 8-19 we see many traits of an apostate. These are traits that we need to watch out for:

1. Dreamers that defile the flesh
2. Reject authority
3. Speaks evil of dignitaries
4. Speak evil of whatever they do not know
5. Corrupt themselves
6. False worship like Cain

7. Greed like Balaam
8. Rejected authority like Korah
9. Without fear of God
10. Serving only themselves
11. Clouds without water
12. Pulled up by the roots
13. Raging waves of the sea
14. Wandering stars
15. Ungodly
16. Grumblers and complainers
17. Walking in their own lusts
18. They know the art of flattery
19. Mockers
20. Cause divisions
21. Not having the Spirit

As Christians, we need to watch out for all these types of traits that we ourselves could stumble on. We are not perfect. When we aren't careful and let sinfulness come in, we can begin to stumble and be influenced by things not of God. I pray we look to the truth in God's Word, look to Jesus, and live to please Him and walk away from anything that will cause division and stop us from growing closer to Him.

Lastly, I pray we can know how to handle these apostates in the right way, giving it over to God and letting him rebuke.

> *Yet Michael the archangel, in contending with the devil, when he disputed about the body of Moses, dared not bring against him a reviling accusation, but said, "The Lord rebuke you!"*
>
> *- Jude 1:9*

In verse 9, we see Michael and his dispute with the devil. There have been many discussions on what the reason for the dispute was. There is no evidence whether they were disputing over Moses' burial or if they were disputing more on the possession of the body of Moses. However, this isn't what we should be focusing on.

Michael the archangel let the Lord rebuke the devil. He dared not to bring against him a reviling accusation. This shows that when dealing with Satan or his helpers, the right course of action is to look to the Lord. We seek His power because we have no power in ourselves. This is the same for apostates. When dealing with false teachers and apostates we must seek after the Lord and His strength. We must go to Him and let Him take charge. He is the one with all power, and He is the final Judge. Sometimes we might feel like apostates and false teachers are getting away with sinful behaviour, but just wait. The Lord sees, and the Lord will judge. Stand on truth and grow in grace.

FIVE

BUILDING YOURSELVES UP ON YOUR MOST HOLY FAITH

> *Jude 1:20*
> *But you, beloved, building yourselves up on your*
> *most holy faith, praying in the Holy Spirit*

Starting at verse 20 of Jude, we see some steps to how we can grow in grace. When we read the phrase "build yourselves up," it sounds like the way to live in this world is to count on yourself. This phrase seems to be focused on all the work that you need to do as opposed to the work of the Lord. However, this is far from the truth. Yes, if you are to grow in Christ you need to get to work. You will need to make sacrifices so that you can be more like Christ. Yet, it is rooted and grounded in the Lord, not you. It involves building on truth and grace. It involves trusting that God will give you the strength if you build on the right things.

Grace isn't just this religious ingredient, or religious element, that we can randomly have. There is someone that is attached to grace. There is a real person who creates a new heart and who puts a new spirit in us. This person is the Lord Jesus Christ. Jesus changes us, and we can be strengthened by being reminded of the grace of the gospel, what Jesus did on that cross for you and for me. We need to be reminded of the gospel daily as we build on our most holy faith.

I remember having a conversation with a young person about the gospel. This person was from the church but unfortunately never lived for Christ. They told me that they felt like the church spent too much time going over the gospel. The gospel was getting old to them. As a younger person in my faith, I didn't really know how to respond to that at the time. However, that conversation stuck with me throughout the years. I pray that nobody has this thought while reading this right now, the thought of the gospel getting old. Our hearts need to be lifted by hearing once again that there is a God who saves weak sinners like me. I pray that the gospel message won't ever get old. If you truly believe, how could it get old?

I don't care if this is your first-time hearing about the gospel, or you have heard it a million times. The gospel should motivate us daily. Let us daily, hourly, be reminded that we serve a God who loves us so much. Let us never go a day without being reminded that God is full of grace and let us never get tired of hearing what Christ has done for us. The message of the gospel should cause a fire within us. A fire that should motivate us to serve Him and to draw closer to Him.

As we look at the idea of working hard in the faith, keep all this in mind. Salvation is not earned. God has given us the strength to live the Christian life. The only real question to ask is this: what are we going to do with what we have been given? Are we going to work hard and keep growing in truth? Or are we going to become lazy and stop growing? That is up to you.

When you think of growing in your Christian walk, having discipline is something every believer needs. Imagine you never brushed your teeth. Imagine you only brushed your teeth the day you had to see your dentist. It would not matter if you brushed your teeth for 2 hours that day, you would still have problems. Your teeth would have cavities, or possibly fall out, and your breath would be unbearable. Brushing your teeth only on that day would not help anything. Yet, doing it twice a day everyday makes your teeth clean. It takes consistency. When it comes to growing in our faith, going to church once a year, once a month, or even once a week will not help you grow the way you should. We should be daily in the Word, daily praying to God, daily looking to Jesus. It takes consistency! It takes discipline!

Jude makes it clear that we need to be grounded and built up on truth. This will also take discipline. One way we do that is by being in His Word, reading the Bible daily. This is so important on many different levels. It's important because we are spending time with the Lord. We are building on our relationship with Him. We also stay busy in the Word because if we are not grounded in truth, we will stray back and forth and will be caught up in the lies of the apostates.

The idea here in Jude 1:20 is that believers will be grounded and built on the Word of God so that when apostates and false teachers come, they will know what truth is. It is the Word of God that we need to turn to and nothing else. It is the Word of God that we build on. It is the Word of God that we are rooted in.

The world has many voices. We can go online and see the opinions of everyone. We can Google something and find arguments that support our own thinking. We can go to Instagram pages and find advice on how to think. We can watch YouTube videos of celebrities and see what they think of a topic or a current event. We also find thousands of podcasts that do the same. There are millions of voices in the world with millions of different viewpoints and opinions. Yet only one voice matters. It is the Lord's. What does the Bible say? What is God saying? We need to follow His Word because that is the truth. And if we are grounded in truth, we won't be easily moved.

An illustration of this is found in Matthew 7 with the story of the wise man building his house on the rock. The rain came and the storm came, yet it did not fall. However, the foolish man who built his house on the sand had a different story. The rain came and the storm came, it blew and beat on the house, and it fell. Matthew 7:27 says "And great was its fall".

Even though Matthew 7 might be talking about salvation, we see many lessons we can take away from this story. One lesson is that if we are grounded and built up on truth, no matter what is thrown our way we will not be moved. Apostates might come, false teachers might come, and yet we won't be fooled because we know what the truth is. We are built on Him who is our rock, who is truth. In contrast, if we listen to the world, if we go to other sources rather than the Bible for answers, we will be like the foolish man. The house may not fall, but it will sway back and forth. It will move left and right not knowing where it should go. The house will be damaged and will result in many problems to fix. When apostates and false teachers come, we will be easily fooled if we don't have a solid foundation.

Do you understand the importance of being in the Word now? If that doesn't show you how important it is, we can go back to the first reason why staying in the Word is so important. It is a time to be with the Lord. As a Christian, we were made to walk in a relationship with Jesus Christ. Being in His Word is a chance to spend time reading what He has said. It is a time to get away from all the world and all the voices it throws at you, and you get to be in truth. Don't ever take that for granted.

Throughout my life I have regretted not taking more time in this busy life to spend it with Him. However, there is not one time I have regretted being in the Word. You will never regret being in the Word of God. You will never regret studying His Word and building on truth. You will never regret growing in Christ. That is one thing you will never regret in this lifetime.

So, we must get to work. We must study and see what Scripture truly says. That is how we won't sway back and forth. That is how we guard against apostates and false teachers. Be in His Word. Stay busy in His Word. Learn His Word. Obey His Word. Stand on truth and grow in grace.

SIX

PRAYING IN THE HOLY SPIRIT

Jude 1:20
But you, beloved, building yourselves up on your
most holy faith, praying in the Holy Spirit

The same verse that says you should build yourselves up on your most holy faith has another hard, yet important, challenge to help us grow in grace. We must pray in the Holy Spirit, but what does that truly mean?

The statement "praying in the Holy Spirit" is a statement that people might have a hard time explaining. Many people pray, but maybe they aren't praying in the Holy Spirit. Maybe they are praying in of their own flesh and desires.

Praying in the Holy Spirit means that the Spirit is moving in their prayers. It means that the prayers are guided to do the will of God and not the will of man. Praying in the Holy Spirit means that you are humbling yourself and letting the Spirit work and not your flesh. In Scripture we see several verses that mention praying in the Holy Spirit including in the book of Ephesians.

> *Praying always with all prayer and supplication in the Spirit.*
>
> *- Ephesians 6:18*

In the previous chapter we talked about building on the foundation of our most holy faith. We need to stand firm on truth and build on the right things. Another way to say it is that we need to put on the armour of God. That is what chapter 6 in Ephesians is talking about before the statement "praying in the Spirit."

The Christian life is a battle and a war against the flesh. We need to put on the whole armour of God and use everything He has given us, including prayer. When you read chapter 6 of Ephesians, notice how it starts off in verse 10 talking about the armour of God.

> *Finally, my brethren, be strong in the Lord and in the power of His might.*
>
> *- Ephesians 6:10*

The idea here is that we need to be strong in the Lord, not ourselves. We need to be reminded that power comes through Him, not ourselves. We need to be reminded that if we are to win against the flesh and against sin, we need to find strength in God. This reminder is needed with prayer as well.

Ephesians 6 mentions the different parts of the armour to help us against the wiles of the devil:

1. The Belt of Truth
2. The Breastplate of Righteousness
3. Footwear of the Gospel of Peace
4. Shield of Faith
5. The Helmet of Salvation
6. The Sword of the Spirit

Often when reading about the many things we need to put on to help us, we stop at the Sword of the Spirit. However, it doesn't stop there. We need number 7: prayer.

As we already read in Ephesians 6:18, we need to pray in the Spirit. This is a daily battle, and we need to daily go to God with prayer to fight against the flesh and the devil.

The times when I do not pray during the day are often the times when I get caught up in what the devil wants me to do. On the other hand, when I do pray, I start to focus on what is important again. When I pray, I am doing so in a humble spirit relying on God's and not my own flesh. That is when I can stand firm in this world.

There are many quotes on the topic of prayer. One might say "you cannot stumble if you are on your knees." How true that is. Prayer should be the first thing a believer does when he or she is in any situation. One must pray, pray, pray, and pray. Martin Luther said "prayer is the most important thing in my life. If I should neglect prayer for a single day, I should lose a great deal of the fire of faith." Don't ever stop praying.

Of course, what makes praying so hard is when sin enters in. There is one illustration that explains this perfectly. It's a story of a child disobeying her parents. When the father discovers this, he begins to question the child about what she had done. The child lost her smile and became distant. The child simply told her father, "I don't want to talk."

Just think back to when you were a child or think about your own child if you have one now. If they disobeyed you as a parent, would they want to talk? Absolutely not. This is the same with God. We know that if we are a born-again believer, we cannot lose our salvation. Yet, sin can break fellowship with God, and we can become distant to Him. Sometimes we don't feel like talking to Him because of our sin. But those are the times we need to talk the most. When we don't feel like praying, we must pray. Pray, pray, pray, and pray.

I've always said that praying is often the easiest thing to do. Yet for me it is also the hardest thing to do. I make praying so hard. Sometimes I think I have too much going on that I don't have time to pray. Sometimes daily life gets in the way and I'm going from one place to another forgetting all that I need to do. We can make so many excuses not to pray. But they are just that, excuses. We have no excuse. We can and should always be in prayer with God. We have no excuses but to spend time with our God. Nobody is as busy as we think we are.

A great example of this is found in the person of Nehemiah. The book of Nehemiah is an amazing book highlighting the importance of prayer. Nehemiah was chosen by God to rebuild the wall of Jerusalem. All throughout the book we see Nehemiah praying and praying. Opposition keeps coming, Nehemiah keeps praying. One example of this is in chapter 2 of Nehemiah. This is when Nehemiah is in front of the king.

> *Then the king said to me, "What do you request?" So*
> *I prayed to the God of heaven.*
> - *Nehemiah 2:4*

Nehemiah is having a conversation with the king. The king sees Nehamiah sad and asks him what is wrong. Nehemiah tells the king that his homeland is destroyed. The king then replies, "What is your request?" Nehemiah's response is truly amazing. Before Nehemiah responds to the king, Nehemiah first prays to God. Although Nehemiah is standing before the king, he has time to pray. We are not sure how long or what type of prayer this is. I picture this prayer as a silent and short prayer to ask God for help what to say. This is a perfect picture of how modern Christians should be praying in the Spirit. We go to God first and ask Him what to say instead of relying on our flesh to respond.

Another verse that helps us understand what praying in the Holy Spirit means is Matthew 6:10: "your kingdom come; your will be done".

If you know Matthew 6, Jesus is teaching the model prayer. In that prayer, He goes on to say, "your kingdom come, your will be done." How do we pray in the Spirit? We humble ourselves, we surrender, and we let the will of God, not our own will, guide us in this life. We pray in accordance with the will of God.

This is a challenging thought to have. Am I praying in the will of God or my own flesh? Am I praying with motives that would just benefit my flesh? Am I listening to the Spirit and putting the will of God first?

In the same way, the Spirit helps us in our weakness.
We do not know what we ought to pray for, but the
Spirit Himself intercedes for us.

- Romans 8:26

Another amazing aspect about prayer is found in Romans 8. When we have the Spirit, He helps us in any situation. When we truly are living through and by the Holy Spirit, the Spirit intercedes for us. The Spirit will help us along, give us words, and protect us from praying with motives that will not benefit the will of God.

Overall, praying in the Holy Spirit means to set aside the flesh and pray in accordance with the will of God. Praying in the Holy Spirit means that we are not just praying a prayer for practice or for religious use. We are praying to the Father as one to whom we surrender all. We are praying to the Father in submission to Him and His will. Stand on truth and grow in grace.

SEVEN

KEEP YOURSELVES IN THE LOVE OF GOD

> *Jude 1:21*
> *keep yourselves in the love of God, looking for the*
> *mercy of our Lord Jesus Christ unto eternal life.*

The next step to growing in grace is found in verse 21 of Jude. Starting in verse 21, Jude has another phrase that one might have a hard time fully understanding. The phrase is, "keep yourselves in the love of God." This phrase has the wording that maybe God would stop loving you. It has the language that maybe you must work for God's love. Yet, we know none of this is true. So, what does "keep yourselves in the love of God" truly mean?

One of the best examples of this idea is going back to the prodigal son. If you remember back in chapter 1, this story is mentioned to show how the son places his identity in another country where he wastes away his possessions. He moves away thinking it is better somewhere else. But realizing it is better with the father, the son knows where his true identity is placed. It is back with the father. The son had been living with the father where he was supposed to be. He had been around the love of the father. Nevertheless, he leaves and finds himself away from the father's love. A place he doesn't belong. What is another lesson we can learn from this? Keep yourselves in the love of God.

One amazing aspect of the prodigal son is how the father never stops loving the son who goes away. It is the same with us and God. God doesn't stop loving us. There might be times in our lives that we stray in this world. We might try so hard to fit into the world that we find ourselves away from God. We try so hard to place our identity in other things rather than knowing our true identity is with the Father. If we are away from the Father, we find ourselves in a place where we no longer can appreciate and enjoy God's love like we should. Why? We are away from true peace.

During this lifetime, we cannot let sin get in the way. Sin has major effects. As believers in Christ, sin can still separate us from enjoying all that God has for us. We cannot lose our salvation, but we can lose joy when we move further and further away from God.

Have you ever been at the beach when there are clouds? You're soaking in the sun and enjoying all that the sun is giving. But what happens when dark clouds come? What happens when a storm covers up the sun? You wouldn't be able to appreciate all that the beach is trying to give you. You couldn't appreciate the sand, the water, or the waves. The sun is still there but the dark clouds have come and covered up the light. It is the same with the love of God and sin. God's love is always there, but sin can rob us of God's glorious light.

Going back to the prodigal son, what happens when the son returns to the Father? Does the Father deny his return? Does he tell him to go away? Absolutely not. The father has compassion, runs, and falls on his neck and kisses him. That is the love of the father. We have a Father who loves us; we have a Father who will never stop loving us. So why do we let sin get in the way of that? Why do we rob ourselves from truly appreciating all that God wants to give us?

Keep yourselves in the love of God! Stay close to Him, be in His Word, daily be in prayer, daily walk with Him.

When we draw closer to Him, we understand more of two things. One, we understand more of our sinful nature. When we draw closer to Him, we understand how much of a sinner we truly are. Two, we understand more of the love of God. We understand more of what He has done for sinners like us. We understand more of the depths of His love, and we appreciate and can enjoy more of who God is. Stay close to the Father's love!

In my own personal life, the times I am struggling with joy, peace, and comfort are the times when I am away from the Lord. The times when I am straying back and forth in this world and being easily tempted are the times when I am not growing in grace.

The idea here of keeping yourselves in the love of God is the understanding that God's love is not what we deserve. We deserve hell, punishment, and the penalty of death. That is why God's love is so special. It is unconditional love. It is full of grace, mercy, and compassion. It is a love that is true and perfect. We need to stay in this love.

Another example of staying in the love of God is in the book of Hosea. Look at Hosea chapter 3 with Gomer. We see how this book is about Israel's sin and rebellion. Hosea will show that God will bring punishment because of their sin. However, the amazing thing about this book and the character of God is that God's love shines through. God is righteous and punishes evil, but God's main goal is to save. He wants all to be saved. The book of Hosea is about God's loyal love.

We see in chapter 1 that God tells Hosea to marry Gomer. Marry a wife of harlotry. Marry someone who is unfaithful. Hosea is faithful to God and does what the Lord told him to do. We then get to chapter 3 of Hosea. Gomer is committing adultery, being sold to the highest bidder. And what do we see Hosea do? He pays for his wife. What would that be like? Watching Hosea pay for Gomer. We are not sure what Gomer was thinking or what she was doing at this moment. However, there must have been shame and a lot of guilt as Hosea pays 15 shekels of silver. Why would Hosea do this? Why would he go to this place of shame and put his heart on the line again for a woman who has been unfaithful time and time again? It must be that Hosea truly loves Gomer. Hosea has loyal love.

You see, this story is a picture of Israel and God. Yet, it is also a picture of us and the Lord. The Lord loves us. We fall into sin, we fail Him, and yet He is still there. Just like Hosea, the Lord had to face humiliation to buy back us.

> *Let this mind be in you, which was also in Christ Jesus, who, being in the form of God, did not consider it robbery to be equal with God, but made Himself of no reputation, taking the form of a bondservant, and coming in the likeness of men. And being found in appearance as a man, He humbled Himself and became obedient to the point of death, even the death of the cross.*
>
> *- Philippians 2:5-8*

God's love is so amazing. He humbled Himself and was humiliated on a cross for you and me. He was beaten and torn. He was mocked. Why would He do this? Why would He save people that have failed over and over again? It must be that He is love. Full of grace and mercy. And the amazing thing about this love is that nothing can separate us from it.

> *For I am persuaded that neither death nor life, nor angels nor principalities nor powers, nor things present nor things to come nor height nor depth, nor any other created thing shall be able to separate us from the love of God which is in Christ Jesus our Lord.*
>
> *- Romans 8:38-39*

There have been times when I have failed or fallen and thought I crossed some invisible line. I went too far. I wonder if Gomer ever thought that as she was being sold. Did she think she went too far? Did she think she played the harlot too many times and it must be over now? Yet Hosea was still there.

This type of love doesn't just go away. God doesn't love us sometimes and then leaves us the next. He is always there, reaching out to those who are lost. Yet, people will turn away from His love. People will reject this love and look to the world to fill it. We can't earn this love, but our response determines how much we enjoy this type of love. Our response is determining if joy is being lost or the cup of joy is being filled up day by day. Stay in the love of God; keep yourselves in His love. How do we do that? Be in His Word, pray in the Spirit, and run to the Father and not this world. Stand on truth and grow in grace.

EIGHT

LOOKING FOR THE MERCY OF OUR LORD JESUS CHRIST

> *Jude 1:21*
> *keep yourselves in the love of God, looking for the*
> *mercy of our Lord Jesus Christ unto eternal life.*

Jude continues to talk about how we grow in grace. We look "for the mercy of our Lord Jesus Christ unto eternal life." The phrase in this verse highlights Christ's return when He will come back and take His bride home. Notice how it says, "unto eternal life." As Christians, this is the hope we hold to. This brings us comfort in a world that is hostile.

Verse 21 also challenges us to stay in the love of God. How do we stay in the love of God? Look at the right things. Focus on what is important. Look for the mercy of the Lord Jesus Christ unto eternal life.

We see an aspect of this in Hebrews 11. We see heroes of the faith looking not to this world but to a heavenly hope. This is something we need to do as we look for the mercy of the Lord Jesus Christ unto eternal life.

> *By faith Abraham obeyed when he was called to go out to the place which he would receive as an inheritance. And he went out, not knowing where he was going. By faith he dwelt in the land of promise as in a foreign country, dwelling in tents with Isaac and Jacob, the heirs with him of the same promise; for he waited for the city which has foundations, whose builder and maker is God.*
>
> *- Hebrews 11:8-10*

Notice in Hebrews 11 how Abraham lived. He first had faith in God, and he showed that faith by going out even though he did not know where he was going. That is true faith. True faith is action. It is taking steps even though you cannot see or understand. You put all trust in God.

Abraham also had faith by waiting for the city whose builder and maker is God. Abraham had full trust in God. Waiting for what God had promised Him. Abraham is just one example of the many of the heroes of faith we see in Hebrews 11.

> *These all died in faith, not having received the promises, but having seen them afar off were assured of them, embraced them and confessed that they were strangers and pilgrims on the earth. For those who say such things declare plainly that they seek a homeland. And truly if they had called to mind that country from which they had come out, they would have had opportunity to return. But now they desire a better, that is, a heavenly country. Therefore, God is not ashamed to be called their God, for He has prepared a city for them.*
>
> *- Hebrews 11:13-16*

For these heroes of faith, they had a heavenly hope. They understood that they were foreigners and pilgrims. They were just visitors on this earth. As Christians, this earth is not our home. Our home is in heaven. We belong with the Father in eternity.

In Hebrews 11:13-16, we see three phrases that change how we should think and live.

1. Strangers and pilgrims
2. Seek a homeland
3. Heavenly country

We are strangers and pilgrims. We do not belong to this world. Why are we trying to please it? Why are we trying to please this world and live like this is our home? We are just passing through. As Christians, we seek a homeland. We know we have a home waiting for us in heaven.

We know that we can become so easily caught up in the things of this world. We focus so much on building a life for ourselves. We focus so much on building the best career possible with the best place to live so we can enjoy retirement. We focus so much on money and status so we can enjoy living out the rest of our lives here on this earth. Of course, working hard is biblical. We must work hard for the glory of God, and in theory that will probably create achievements in our work life. We know getting a great job and being successful in our work is a great thing. However, what gain do we have if we don't know and are not in the will of God? Why would we place those things above God? Can we take it all with us? Absolutely not! Look to eternal life and make sure you build on the right things. We have a heavenly country!

In Philippians, Paul talks about how a Christian's citizenship is not a country or a region here on earth. For the believer, his citizenship is in heaven.

For our citizenship is in heaven, from which we also
eagerly wait for the Savior, the Lord Jesus Christ.
- Philippians 3:20

For those who put their faith and trust in God, heaven is our country. For those living in the United States of America, that is not your country. For those living in Brazil, that is not your country. For those living in New Zealand, that is not your country. For those living in China, that is not your country. Can we fully understand that?

No matter where you live on this earth as believers in Christ, it won't be your home. You have one home. You have one country that you belong to. It is with the Father; it is with Him in heaven. This should give you comfort for the future but also motivation on how you should live on this earth.

> *Rejoice in the Lord always. Again, I will say, rejoice!*
> *Let your gentleness be known to all men. The Lord is*
> *at hand. Be anxious for nothing, but in everything by*
> *prayer and supplication, with thanksgiving, let your*
> *requests be made known to God; and the peace of God,*
> *which surpasses all understanding, will guard your*
> *hearts and minds through Christ Jesus.*
> *- Philippians 4:4-7*

After Paul writes that our citizenship is in heaven, Paul writes how believers should live on this earth. We should live differently than the world. We see in chapter 4 verses 4-7 that a citizen of heaven rejoices, despite the circumstances. A citizen of heaven is gracious and gentle. A citizen of heaven prays instead of worrying. This is easier said than done. However, as Christians if we know we are secure in Him, why worry? Why wouldn't we be gracious? Why wouldn't we be gentle? If we truly are a citizen of heaven, we will live differently.

A hymn that comes to mind when thinking about our heavenly citizenship is a hymn called "We Have a Home Above". A song written by Henry Bennett in the 1800's.

"We have a home above, from all defilement free; a mansion which eternal love prepared our rest to be. The Father's gracious hand has built that blest abode; from everlasting it was planned, the dwelling place of God."

We have a home! As we wait for the Lord, and as we wait to be with God in heaven, we must be examples of Jesus. When the world complains, we rejoice. When the world is angry and full of rage, we are gracious and gentle. When the world is worried, we pray. Because of the gracious gift of God, we have been made new; we are now citizens of heaven. The world should see something different.

I grew up going to church and I have seen great examples of how people live like citizens of heaven. Unfortunately, I've also seen bad examples of how people should be living if they are citizens of heaven. But when I look back at the great examples, I am encouraged. I am blessed to have those people in my life. People that show gentleness, graciousness, forgiveness, love, humility.

You must understand that a preacher can speak on how to be a citizen of heaven and a Bible scholar can write about how we have a heavenly hope; we can be encouraged by this. However, I have learned a lot more from the uneducated, simple man who lives out this faith daily. That shows what true humility is, that shows gentleness, in any circumstance. I have learnt more about Jesus from people who aren't leaders in a church, more than pastors and elders. So, you might have a great biblical education. You might be placed in a high position at your local church, but do you live like you're a citizen of heaven? Do you live it out? This heavenly hope should bring us both comfort and motivation through this life.

For the Lord Himself will descend from heaven with a shout, with the voice of an archangel, and with the trumpet of God. And the dead in Christ will rise first. Then we who are alive and remain shall be caught up together with them in the clouds to meet the Lord in the air. And thus, we shall always be with the Lord. Therefore comfort one another with these words.
- 1 Thessalonians 4:16-18

We can hold on to these words as pilgrims and strangers on this earth. We wait for the moment we will meet the Lord in the air. What comfort it brings us when we read "we shall always be with the Lord." How amazing is that?! No more pain, no more tears, and no more sin. We will be in heaven with God for all of eternity.

So, as we live in this world, as we battle against apostates and false teachers, as we are surrounded by the enemy, hold on to this. Hold on and be comforted by the thought that this is not our home. The Lord is coming back. Look for the mercy of our Lord Jesus Christ unto eternal life. Stand on truth and grow in grace.

NINE

MOVE WITH CAUTION

> *Jude 1:22-23*
> *And on some have compassion, making a distinction;*
> *but others save with fear, pulling them out of the fire,*
> *hating even the garment defiled by the flesh.*

The book of Jude so far has communicated to us what an apostate is, how to handle these apostates, and how we should stand on truth and grow in grace. Jude then gives us a big warning. We must move with caution.

Here Jude is writing about people who have fallen and stumbled because of apostates. These are people who have fallen for the enemy and their lies. Some will need more gentleness while others need a harder influence to pull them out. This is an example of making a distinction. It is the way and manner of helping another. So why should we move with caution?

Jude is giving us a big warning to move with caution, so you won't be pulled down when trying to help another. As Christians we should be focused on helping people who have fallen. We should do this by going to the Word, showing them truth, and praying for them. As we have seen in Jude there are different ways to handle these challenges; that is why we need to make a distinction. There are some who have fallen heavily in the things of an apostate. We need to be careful that we don't fall as well.

This shows how powerful sin is. As Christians, we have the Holy Spirit. We have been born again. Yet we sometimes forget that sin still has power as we battle with the flesh. We must understand that nothing can separate us from eternity with God, but sin has the power to damage our relationship with Him. Sin has the power to destroy relationships with others, and sin has the power to make us live for this world without us even realizing how far we have strayed from the path of God.

Have you ever done something you said you would never do? Have you ever committed a sin and asked "How did I ever get to this point?" For many, this is the case. The sin starts small and gets bigger and bigger. We don't understand that any sin has a big influence on how we live. We don't understand that we can slip at any moment if we stop focusing on Christ and don't look to the Word. That is why we need to have caution when dealing with those who have fallen. If we are not careful, we will stumble too. As we help others, we open the door to be influenced by what they were influenced by. That is why we need to stand on truth and keep growing in grace. We need to keep our eyes on Him.

We must take these situations seriously. We must ask for wisdom from God to handle what is thrown at us. This can be applied to everything we have talked about throughout this book. We need to take this Christian life seriously and move with caution in every part of our life.

If we don't take our identity seriously, we will find identity in this world. We will start to live for this world and believe what the world thinks about us and not what God thinks. We will become slaves of this world and not bondservants of Christ.

If we don't take contending for the faith seriously, we will start to allow threats to creep into the church. We will start to allow the power of sin to change the church. It will create opportunities for apostates and false teachers to influence others and change what we view as truth.

If we don't take building ourselves up in our most holy faith seriously, we will start listening to the thoughts of man. We will start to build on the wrong things to the point that we will start to sway back and forth. We will be influenced by anything that comes our way.

If we don't take praying in the Spirit seriously, we will start to pray with wrong motives. We will start to pray with pride and focus on what we want and not the will of God. We will start to live outside of the will of God.

If we don't take keeping ourselves in the love of God seriously, we will let sin in, joy will be depleted, and we won't experience the love of God like we should.

If we don't take looking for the mercy of our Lord Jesus Christ unto eternal life seriously, we will stop focusing on heavenly things, and we will focus on this world. We will start to build on things of this world and not heavenly rewards.

Lastly, if we don't deal with people who have fallen seriously, we could stumble and fall ourselves. We need to take every part of our Chrisitan walk seriously. We must move with caution throughout our life here on this earth. We need to look to God for all things because if we don't, we will start to look for answers in this world. We will stand on the wrong things and grow in things that are rubbish.

> *Therefore, take careful heed to yourselves, that you love the Lord your God.*
>
> *- Joshua 23:11*

> *See then that you walk circumspectly, not as fools but as wise, redeeming the time, because the days are evil. Therefore, do not be unwise, but understand what the will of the Lord is.*
>
> *- Ephesians 5:15-17*

> *Therefore, let him who thinks he stands take heed lest he fall.*
>
> *- 1 Corinthians 10:12*

These are a handful of verses showing that we need to move with caution, carefully watching where we stand. We need daily prayer to God to ask for strength to move through this life. We need wisdom to understand what is from God and what will draw us away from Him.

As we move with caution, we also need to consider what we are focusing on.

> *Set your mind on things above, not on things on the earth.*
>
> *- Colossians 3:2*

What we focus on grows. If I give all my focus to sports, my knowledge and abilities will start to grow in the sport I am focused on. If I give all my focus to school, my knowledge and abilities will start to grow in the classes and courses I am in. What we focus on grows. This is the same with our relationship with the Lord Jesus Christ. Our minds, thoughts, and hearts should be pointing to one name, Jesus!

After Paul writes about setting your mind on things above in Colossians, he goes on to talk about the new man. If you have faith in the Lord Jesus Christ, believing in the power of the cross, then you have been created new. We have become citizens of heaven. Our focus now must be on things above and not on the old life before Christ.

Our relationship with the Lord is the most important thing we could ever have. Focusing on this world will only give you temporary satisfaction. It will only give you temporary pleasures that lead to destruction. We must focus on Jesus, who gives us true peace and comfort as we rest in the grace of Jesus Christ. We must focus on things above and move with caution while living in this world, a world full of sin. Stand on truth and grow in grace.

TEN

GIVE ALL GLORY TO GOD

Jude 1:24-25
Now to Him who is able to keep you from stumbling, and
to present you faultless before the presence of His glory with
exceeding joy, To God our Savior, who alone is wise, Be glory and
majesty, Dominion and power, Both now and forever. Amen.

The book of Jude ends with a powerful message to all of us. These last few verses put everything in perspective. It is God who deserves the glory. It is God from whom we receive all power. It is God who alone is wise. It is because of God that we are presented faultless, and it is God who keeps us from stumbling. What a Saviour we have!

How do we go through situations so that we do not stumble? What is the answer when we are faced with opposition and challenges? The simple answer is God. He alone keeps us from stumbling. To guard against apostates we must lean on the Word, and lean on God.

No matter how hard life may seem and no matter how difficult the opposition may look, if we trust in God we won't stumble. We won't fall. He has given us His Word and the Holy Spirit to guide us through anything we face.

> *I have taught you in the way of wisdom; I have led you in right paths. When you walk, your steps will not be hindered, And when you run, you will not stumble.*
>
> *- Proverbs 4:11-12*

We see in Proverbs that when we run we will not stumble. Notice how it says "run". As believers in Christ, we are running a race. Unfortunately, as we run this race, we still have the flesh. We are going to go through temptations and opposition that will influence us to stumble. Yet with the help of God, He alone can keep us from stumbling. He leads us. This is important to understand. We must let Him lead. We must let Him take control of our lives. We need to trust, follow, and obey Him. When we can do that, we won't stumble. We will know the truth and we won't be fooled by apostates and false teachers.

But God's promise that He will keep us from stumbling doesn't stop there. In Jude 24 it goes on to say,

And to present you faultless before the presence of His glory with exceeding joy.

Before Christ, the words to describe myself would be dead, blind, a slave to sin, and an enemy of God. Yet how amazing it is to read in Jude that He will present me faultless before the presence of His glory. I deserve the deepest parts of hell. I deserve all the punishment that Jesus took on the cross. I am guilty. I have fallen short of God's glory. All this is true, but He will present me faultless.

> *being justified freely by His grace through the redemption that is in Christ Jesus.*
>
> *- Romans 3:24*

I am alive. I can see. I am free. I am a child of God because of the cross. I can now be presented as faultless before the presence of His glory not because of anything I did, but because of what He has done for me. It is all because of the love, grace, and mercy of Jesus Christ. It is all because of the work done at the cross. This brings true joy!

Some may say that Jude 24 is talking about the joy we have when presented faultless. However, the wording here seems to be talking about the joy God will have.

Both believers and God will have joy. Yet this verse seems to be focused on the joy He will have. It brings God joy. It brings Him joy seeing one of His children coming home. It brings Him joy seeing one of His children who was dead now alive. It brings Him joy seeing us out of the bondage of sin, and it brings Him joy that He can present us faultless to Himself.

I am reminded once again of the story of the prodigal son. What happens when the son comes home? The father has compassion, runs, and falls on his neck and kisses him. What a beautiful scene. What joy the father must have had when he saw his own son coming home. What joy the father must have had when he could run to him and kiss him. This is the picture I see when God presents us faultless. It blows my mind thinking about our wonderful Saviour.

The last verse in Jude goes on to say that our God is our Saviour who alone is wise. Is the world wise? Are apostates wise? Are false teachers wise? We go to God who alone is wise. He has all the answers. He has all understanding. He alone is the source for truth.

If God is the one who keeps us from stumbling, presents us faultless, and is the source of wisdom, to whom should we give glory? If we give any glory to things outside of God, we have bought the lie of this world. The lie that worldly possessions and objects matter over God. We have focused on ourselves and man's teachings rather than focusing on the one true answer. We cannot live this way. We should give all glory and praise to God the Father.

> *Let everything that has breath praise the Lord. Praise the Lord!*
>
> *- Psalms 150:6*

As we go through this life no matter the circumstances, let us praise God with everything we have, with everything we say, and with everything we do. He has given us so much. He is our Saviour. He is our rock. He is the one who keeps us from stumbling. He is the one who will present us faultless. The least we can do on this earth is live for Him and praise Him with everything we have.

> *Praise the Lord, all you Gentiles! Laud Him, all you peoples! For His merciful kindness is great toward us, And the truth of the Lord endures forever. Praise the Lord!*
>
> *- Psalm 117*

When talking about praising God, I am reminded of Psalm 117. Not only is Psalm 117 the shortest Psalm, but it is also the shortest chapter in all the bible. Although there are only two verses, this Psalm has a very strong message. First, we see that we should praise the Lord. Second, we see some of the reasons why we should praise the Lord. We should always praise the Lord. We should praise Him in great times, in bad times, in times of uncertainty, and in times of peace. We should praise Him always for who He is and what He has done.

We read that His merciful kindness is great towards us. This right here is a strong and big reason to praise the Lord. I remember a conversation I had back in high school. This young man started talking about how he could never go to church. He thought he did too many bad things to be saved. He could not believe that there is a God full of mercy, grace, and love like our God. He missed the whole point of the cross! God does exist. His love is real. His grace is true. His mercy is everlasting. We have a God that is full of mercy, and His truth will endure forever. Praise the Lord!

As Christians the hard challenge is praising God through trials and sufferings. I know those days when you feel like all this weight is pulling you down and you don't feel like yourself sometimes. I know the days where the problems seem overwhelming. How do we give glory to God and praise Him through it all? Better yet, how do we go through this life with all these apostates, false teachers, and corruption? How can we do it with joy? How do we find peace in a world that is against the truth? Remember the words in Psalm 28.

The Lord is my strength and my shield; My heart trusted in Him, and I am helped; Therefore, my heart greatly rejoices, And with my song I will praise Him.

- Psalm 28:7

We simply trust in who God says He is. When we remember who God is, we find joy and motivation to praise Him. The circumstances around us might be bad, and the trials might keep coming, but those who trust in who God is and His promises will find peace and joy. That is how we praise through it all. We remind ourselves of who He is and claim the promise that He is always with us.

I challenge you all to read the life of Joseph in Genesis. This man had many ups and downs. His brothers plotted to kill him, he was thrown in a pit, he was sold as a slave, and he was put in prison. Although all of this happened, Joseph came to power. Pharaoh set him as ruler over all the land of Egypt. Joseph's circumstances were always changing. However, one thing never changed: God was always with him.

In Genesis chapter 39, we see the phrase "The Lord was with Joseph" multiple times. Through every circumstance God was with him. Like it or not, our circumstances will always change. There will be great times ahead, but unfortunately there will be more challenging times. If you let your circumstances control your joy or peace, you are doomed to fail. You can have comfort and peace knowing that through the good or bad, God is with you. If you are a true believer in Christ, He lives in you. Praise the Lord!

Standing on truth and growing in grace is challenging when living in this world. But when we are reminded of who God is, we find comfort and peace. Will it be easy? No! Yet we must remember these words in Galatians chapter 6.

And let us not grow weary while doing good, for in due season we shall reap if we do not lose heart.

- Galatians 6:9

People around us might be living for this world. People around us might be apostates and false teachers. People around us might be living in sin. What should we do? Keep going! Keep building yourselves up on your most holy faith. Keep praying in the Holy Spirit. Keep yourselves in the love of God. Keep looking for the mercy of our Lord Jesus Christ unto eternal life. No matter what comes your way, remain faithful. Stand on truth and grow in grace.

Printed in the United States
by Baker & Taylor Publisher Services